I0621284

DON'T TALK ABOUT IT, BE ABOUT IT

A Straightforward Path to the Life You Know
You're Meant to Live

GARRICK GRIFFIN

DEDICATION

I wouldn't be here writing these words, coaching these truths, and walking this mission without two giants in my life: my mother, Mrs. Paulette Griffin Sabree, and my grandfather, Mr. Paul Griffin.

Their strength built mine. This book lives in their memory. I hope it makes them proud.

ACKNOWLEDGMENTS

No mission is fulfilled alone. This book, this journey, was never meant to be a solo climb.

To my wife and daughter: Thank you for being my unwavering source of truth, laughter, and love. You hold me steady when things shake and challenge me when I drift. Your belief in me is the rhythm behind every page.

To Ms. Paulette, my mother: You never told me what I wanted to hear; you told me what I needed to hear. Your truth became my compass. Even now, your voice pushes me forward, and your strength holds me upright. Thank you for always believing in me and reminding me that "I can't" was never an option. I can hear you now: "You can do anything you put your mind to."

To my Monday, Wednesday, and Friday morning crew: Thank you for the check-ins, the fire, and the follow-through. And most of all, thank you for pushing me to put all those talks on paper so the world could see. This book exists because you believed the message mattered.

To The Council: What started during a global shutdown became a global connection. No egos. No masks. Just iron sharpening iron, year after year.

To my military family, those I served with, and those still in the fight: You taught me structure, resilience, and purpose. These pages are forged from those lessons. This one is for every Soldier who came home determined to lead in a new way.

To every mentor, friend, listener, and reader who ever said, "Keep going," thank you. This is not just my story. It is *ours*.

And to you, the one holding this book right now: You are not here by accident. Something brought you to these words. Something in you is ready.

Do not wait. Do not stall. *Do not just talk about it, be about it.*

TABLE OF CONTENTS

PREFACE

I didn't write this book to impress you.

I wrote it to remind you of who you are, what you're capable of, and what you no longer have to settle for.

This isn't a textbook. You won't need a dictionary to get through it. I kept it simple, and I did that on purpose. Clarity creates action, and I don't want you to just read this book. I want you to move because of it.

I'm not a philosopher. I'm a product of lived experience. Raised in Birmingham, Alabama, in a single-parent household with my brother, I didn't grow up with much. But I grew up with enough: enough love, enough support, and a mindset that told me the odds were real but beatable.

I joined the Army in 1990. What started as a decision to serve evolved into a 30+ year journey of leadership, discipline, and growth. I've learned that leadership isn't about titles. It's about showing up. And motion beats motivation every time.

This book was born from early morning talks, live social media posts, late-night reflections, and friends who kept saying, "You need to write this down." So, I did. Maybe this found you at a turning point. If it did, I hope it moves you forward with power and clarity.

No fluff. No formulas. Just a straight path to progress.

You're not alone.

You're not stuck.

You're not waiting on perfect.

You're already ready.

Let's stop talking about it.

Let's go get it.

Let's be about it.

Garrick

INTRODUCTION

Turning Intentions into Action

"You don't have to be great to start, but you have to start to be great." — **Zig Ziglar**

Have you ever promised yourself you'd make a change? Perhaps you aimed to go back to school, commit to a healthier lifestyle, or finally chase that dream, only to realize months later that nothing has changed?

You're not alone.

The truth is that a spark of intention can burn bright… then quietly flicker out. And when it does, it often leaves behind frustration, disappointment, and self-doubt.

But it doesn't have to end there.

As a Drill Sergeant Instructor in the U.S. Army, I learned a lesson that reshaped my perspective. Each training cycle, our groups would create a motto to guide them through the hard days. One of those mottos stuck with me more than any other:

"Don't talk about it, be about it."

Six words. Not just a slogan; it's a mindset. A challenge to every excuse, every fear, and every delay. It's also the foundation for this book.

So, what does it actually mean to *be about it*?

It means building habits that drive momentum. It means breaking goals into small, manageable steps. It means celebrating milestones, no matter how minor. It means surrounding yourself with people who lift you up and push you forward. And it means embracing a mindset rooted in grit, gratitude, and growth.

If you've ever felt stuck between who you are and who you know you could be, this book is for you.

There's no fluff here. No jargon. No formulas. Just practical tools, real-life stories, and hard-earned lessons designed to help you close the gap between intention and execution.

By opening this book, you've already taken a step most people won't. You've entered the journey.

The chapters ahead won't just challenge how you think; they'll call you to move.

Let's stop talking about change. Let's start choosing it. Let's get to work. And while you're at it... *Be about it.*

CHAPTER ONE

WHY PEOPLE STRUGGLE TO ACT ON THEIR PLANS AND GOALS

"Vision without action is a daydream. Action without vision is a nightmare." — **Japanese Proverb**

You set a goal. At first, the fire burns strongly. You're energized, motivated, and ready to go. But as the days roll on, that fire begins to fizzle. Before long, you're stuck in the same place, wondering why nothing's changed.

Sound familiar? You're not broken; you're human.

Over the years, I've seen this pattern in myself and in others. And through that lens, I've uncovered a handful of barriers that quietly derail progress. Let's walk through those roadblocks, then begin building the bridge beyond them.

The Comfort Zone Dilemma

One of the biggest reasons people hesitate to act is simple:

they don't want to leave their comfort zone.

That comfort zone is cozy. Familiar. Safe. But real growth lives outside of it.

In the book *Who Moved My Cheese?* by Dr. Spencer Johnson, four characters face sudden change. Two of them embrace it and find new opportunities. The other two resist and remain stuck. That story holds a mirror up to us — we often trade long-term growth for short-term comfort.

However, progress demands discomfort. Your future isn't waiting inside the lines you've already drawn.

The Fear Factor

Fear is a master of disguise. It shows up as procrastination, overthinking, and avoidance, and it stalls our dreams.

Sometimes, it whispers:

- "You're not ready."
- "You'll mess this up."
- "Just wait a little longer…"

I experienced this firsthand. For years, I delayed becoming a Drill Sergeant because of one thing: a fear of heights. Victory Tower, a 34-foot rappel tower, was part of the training.

I had completed it in basic training before, but now the fear had grown louder.

But here's the truth: you don't beat fear by waiting. It backs down when you move.

Unclear Goals or Overwhelming Ambitions

Big goals sound inspiring:

"I'm going to buy a home."

"I'll go back to school."

"I'll save $10,000."

These are great goals, but without a roadmap, they can feel impossible. If you don't break a big dream into steps, overwhelm can sneak in and steal your momentum.

Instead of saying, "I'll save $10,000," what if you said, "I'll save $200 a month"?

Now it's not a mountain. It's a series of steps.

Perfectionism and All-or-Nothing Thinking

Let me be real. I've been guilty of this. For years, I dreamed of starting my own business, but I got stuck in planning mode. I thought every piece had to be perfect before I began.

Meanwhile, others were moving forward, learning as they went. Their progress wasn't flawless, but it was progress. Mine was just potential. Done is better than perfect. Start messy. Learn fast. Keep going.

Competing Priorities and Time Management

Life pulls in every direction:

- Family
- Work
- Unexpected obligations

And suddenly, your personal goals drift to the bottom of the list.

I've been there. I delayed going back to school, building a business, and chasing dreams because I was pouring myself into helping others. That's honorable, but it also cost me time I could have spent becoming who I was meant to be.

You must protect time for your purpose. The world will take what you offer, but time won't give itself to you. You have to claim it.

Lack of Accountability or Support

Some environments lift you up, while others pull you down.

The "crab in a bucket" story paints the picture clearly: one crab tries to escape, and the others drag it back in. It's the same with people. If your circle discourages your growth, progress becomes even harder.

But let me tell you, you don't need permission to grow. What you need is belief, and sometimes a new circle that reflects the future you're working toward, not the past you're leaving behind.

Closing Thoughts

The gap between dreams and results is not talent. It's not luck. It's the decision to act, even when it's scary.

If you've recognized your own roadblocks in these pages, good. Awareness is power. You can't fix what you refuse to face. But now you've faced it. And that makes you dangerous to everything that once held you back.

This isn't just a list of reasons we stall out; it's a mirror, a map, and a wake-up call.

- Comfort only offers temporary relief.
- Fear is just noise.
- Big goals = small steps repeated consistently.
- Perfection is a myth we stop chasing.
- Time is a resource you get to protect. Support isn't optional; it's strategic.

From here, we shift: from stuck to starting, from passive to purposeful.

This book won't move for you. But it will move *with* you.

The world doesn't need more dreamers. It needs more doers.

So, let's *Be about it.*

Reflection & Action

Recognizing Your Gaps:
Insight leads to impact. Start here.

1. What is the most significant obstacle preventing you from acting on your goals?

_____

_____

_____

_____

2. How does staying in your comfort zone impact your progress?

_____

_____

_____

_____

3. What is one goal you've been meaning to pursue but haven't acted on yet? What do you think has been holding you back?

_____

_____

_____

_____

_____

4. How would your life improve if you took just one step toward that goal?

_____

_____

_____

_____

CHAPTER TWO

BREAKING OUT OF THE COMFORT ZONE

"Consider it pure joy… whenever you face trials…
because you know that the testing of your faith
produces perseverance." – **James 1:2–3**

Why do so many people struggle to reach their potential? One reason might surprise you: it's not laziness or lack of ambition, it's comfort. It feels safe, familiar, and controllable. But growth doesn't speak the language of comfort; it speaks risk, courage, and change.

I think about that famous line from *The Wizard of Oz*: "There's no place like home." It's true, but Dorothy didn't discover her strength by staying put. It was the journey away from home, the friends she met, and the obstacles she faced that gave her the confidence and courage to grow.

My own journey began one month out of high school. I was a kid from a low-income neighborhood, raised by a single parent, with no clear direction, except I knew one thing: I needed change. I was surrounded by the same streets, the same people, the same routines. And deep down, I knew that if I stayed... I'd stay stuck.

With my childhood friend hyping me up, shout out to Chris, I walked into an Army recruiter's office. That was the scariest thing I'd done up to that point, but stepping out of my comfort zone that day changed everything. I proudly served in the U.S. Army for over 30 years. I traveled the world, earned multiple degrees, and built relationships that will last me a lifetime, all because I decided to move forward instead of staying still.

You can, too.

Now, let's break it down with practical strategies to help you step out of your comfort zone and into growth.

Start Small

The biggest mistake people make when chasing change is trying to leap instead of taking one step at a time.

For years, I dreamed of writing a book, but the thought of

completing the whole thing overwhelmed me. I stayed stuck, not because I lacked passion, but because I didn't know how to begin.

Eventually, I stopped thinking about the book. I focused on one paragraph. One page. One chapter. And that shift changed everything.

Start small. One habit. One action. One brave decision. The version of you you're becoming isn't built overnight; it's shaped in moments just like this.

Visualize Yourself on the Other Side

Years ago, a friend and I would grab lunch and drive through this new neighborhood, watching as they laid fresh concrete for the foundations, model homes, and manicured lawns. We'd sit there in his car with two-piece chicken dinners, dreaming, "One day, we'll live here."

We couldn't afford it at the time, but that didn't stop us from picturing it.

That vision became fuel, not for fantasy, but for forward motion. Does the dream still feel distant? Get closer to it.

- Walk the campus.

- Sit in the car.

- Tour the house.

- Stand in the place you plan to claim.

What you see, you begin to believe. And what you believe, you start to chase.

There's Nothing to Fear but Fear Itself

So, what's stopping most people from leaving their comfort zone? You already know: fear.

But fear often isn't about what's in front of you. It's about what could happen. It's about the "what-ifs." It's about playing out a movie in your mind where everything goes wrong.

Let's flip that. What if everything goes right? What if the version of you that shows up on the other side is wiser, freer, and finally at peace with the choice to grow? What if fear is just a shadow cast by the light of who you're becoming?

That's exactly what happened to me when I walked into that recruiter's office. That single act shifted the entire direction of my life.

It's okay to feel fear. Just don't let it chain you to a version of yourself you've already outgrown.

Closing Thoughts

You don't have to uproot your whole life, but you do have to disrupt the comfort that's been holding you back.

Growth doesn't happen standing still. It happens in motion. And yes, stepping out of your comfort zone will feel unfamiliar and uncomfortable. But on the other side of discomfort, you find a stronger, freer, and more capable version of the person reading this right now.

You were never meant to grow inside the lines. Stop allowing people to put you in boxes.

Growth and comfort cannot co-exist. True growth begins where comfort ends. You just need to take one step beyond your safety net.

That next step? You already know what it is.

You don't need another sign.

You need a decision.

You've taken a step beyond comfort, and now you're staring at the next obstacle: fear.

This is where most people stop. They dip their toes into growth, feel the chill of uncertainty, and retreat to safety. But not you. You're still here. Still turning pages. Still choosing movement over stillness.

The next chapter isn't just about identifying fear; it's about dismantling it because fear loses power when we stop avoiding it and start approaching it head-on.

You've shaken off comfort. Now let's face fear. *It's time to Be about it.*

Reflection & Action

Your Comfort Zone Challenge

Before turning the page, pause. This is where self-aware-ness becomes power. You've already stepped out; now, challenge yourself to go deeper.

1. What area of your life have you been holding back in because it feels safe or familiar?

_____

_____

_____

_____

2. What opportunities might open if you stepped outside of that comfort zone, even a little?

_____

_____

_____

_____

3. When was the last time you took a leap that scared you, and what did you learn from it?

_____

_____

_____

_____

4. Visualize yourself on the other side of your comfort zone. What do you see? What's different?

_____

_____

_____

_____

CHAPTER THREE

CONFRONTING FEAR

"Everything you've ever wanted is sitting on the other side of fear." — **George Addair**

To confront something, you have to name it, understand it, and strip away its power. Let's start with what fear really is.

Fear is a natural emotional response to perceived danger, whether real or imagined. At its core, fear is a signal. It's our mind's way of preparing us for potential harm, failure, or discomfort. But left unchecked, fear doesn't protect us; it paralyzes us. It becomes a barrier between who we are and who we're meant to be.

In the last chapter, I told you how my fear of heights nearly stopped me from achieving one of my biggest goals: becoming a Drill Sergeant. What's wild is that I'd already faced that same fear during basic training and succeeded. But fear has a way of lingering, even when logic says otherwise. It's natural to be afraid of the unknown, but we cannot allow that fear to stand in the way of becoming the person we promised ourselves we'd be.

So, how do we confront and tame our fears?

Let's walk through it, one courageous step at a time.

Name It to Tame It

What are you afraid of?

You'd be surprised how many people struggle to answer that. They know fear is there, but they can't quite put a finger on it. One of the first steps toward freedom is naming that fear.

When I admitted I was afraid of heights, I finally had something to confront. From there, I could dig deeper: Am I afraid I'll fall and get hurt? That the rope might snap? That I'll embarrass myself?

Right now, pause. Whisper it, write it, speak it aloud, whatever helps you own it. You deserve to name what's been naming you.

- Is it the fear of failure?
- Of rejection?

- Of not being good enough?

The moment you give your fear a name, you strip it of mystery, and you start reclaiming your power.

Reframe the Narrative

Once you've named your fear, it's time to shift the lens.

Ask yourself: What's on the other side of this fear?

For me, overcoming my fear of heights meant becoming a Drill Sergeant. That role allowed me to mentor others who faced the same fear. Time and again, I've found that every fear I've faced stood squarely between me and a goal I deeply cared about.

What if that fear isn't blocking the path, but revealing it? What if naming your fear helps you see the next right step instead of the whole staircase?

Fear is often just your growth in disguise.

Small Steps, Big Courage

You know that old saying: How do you eat an elephant? One bite at a time.

We often fear things because we try to tackle them all at

once. But courage grows in increments. When I was preparing to rappel off that high tower, I didn't start at the top. First, I learned how to tie knots, build a harness, and navigate lower obstacles. Each step built my confidence until the big moment came. What small step can you take today?

Courage isn't the absence of fear; it's proof that we're still moving in spite of it. Break your fear down. Celebrate progress. Let each small win pave the path to your breakthrough.

Visualize the Outcome

One of my favorite movies is *The Waterboy*. Bobby Boucher, a gentle, misunderstood guy, surprises everyone with his hidden football talent, unleashed through pure visualization. His coach asked him to picture someone who made him angry and channel that energy on the field.

Now, I'm not saying you should go tackle anyone, that's fiction, but the takeaway is real: your mind responds to what it sees, even before it happens. Paint your victory in detail, then step into it.

When I saw myself conquering my fear, I imagined standing tall in that Drill Sergeant hat, shaping the future of young men and women, just as my drill sergeant once did for me.

Close your eyes. What do you look like on the other side of your fear? Hold onto that image. Let it drive you.

Embrace the "What Ifs"—Then Redirect

How many times have you stopped yourself because of the "what if" game?

What if I fail?

What if people laugh?

What if I'm not enough?

I've played that game too many times to count. And here's what I've learned: our energy flows where our thoughts go. If we dwell on failure, our actions will be driven by fear. However, if we focus on success and even visualize it, we redirect that energy toward something greater. Fear plays tricks with possibility. But your mind can't tell the difference between imagined disaster and imagined success— unless you teach it.

So, the next time fear whispers, "What if you fall?" answer it boldly: "But what if I soar?"

Find a Battle Buddy

In the military, you're assigned a battle buddy, someone you're accountable to, and who's accountable to you. You learn together. You grow together. You face your fears... together.

You don't have to enlist to understand the value in that.

My grandfather used to say, *"Closed mouths don't get fed."* How does someone know you need help if you don't say anything?

When fear pressed against me, whether it was writing this book or facing real-life decisions, it was friends, fellow authors, and mentors who gave me momentum. When we invite others into our journey, we multiply strength and borrow belief until it becomes our own.

Courage is contagious. Healing is, too.

Find a battle buddy who will tell you what you *need* to hear, not just what you *want* to hear.

Closing Thoughts

Fear will always be part of the journey, but it doesn't have to be the driver.

You can tame it. You can redirect it. You can rise above it.

So, here's your mission right now:

- Name your fear.
- Reframe your story.
- Take one small step.
- Visualize the win.
- Flip the script on "what if."
- Find your battle buddy.

You've named it. Faced it. Stepped through it. You've proved that fear is not a wall; it's a doorway.

Now, let's build new ground: firm habits, clear purpose, bold intention, because movement without direction can still lead to stagnation. Next up, we plan. We build. We move with meaning.

Fear may still whisper. But freedom has a louder voice.

So, lace up your courage… And let's *Be about it.*

Reflection & Action

Facing Fear With Intention

Before you move on, pause here. You've just uncovered how to confront fear; now it's time to face it, in your own words.

1. What fear has been whispering to you most often lately? Give it a name.

_____

_____

_____

_____

2. How has this fear held you back from becoming who you want to be?

_____

_____

_____

_____

3. What could happen if you reframed your fear as a doorway instead of a wall?

_____

_____

_____

_____

4. Think about someone you trust. Who could be your "battle buddy" on this journey, and how can they support you?

_____

_____

_____

_____

CHAPTER FOUR

GOAL SETTING MADE SIMPLE: HOW TO DEFINE CLEAR, ACHIEVABLE GOALS

"Plans are nothing; planning is everything."

– Dwight D. Eisenhower

"Set goals," they say. But what does that really mean?

Too often, we declare we want to "be successful," "get in shape," or "level up," but without a clear target, those intentions drift. They become wishes in disguise, hoping movement will happen without a map.

In the Army, we were trained to execute missions with specificity: clear objectives, measurable milestones, timelines, and intent. You didn't just move; you knew where, why, and how success would be tracked. That kind of clarity? It makes hesitation impossible.

It's the same in life.

Years ago, I told myself, "I want to write a book." But I wasn't making progress. Why? Because saying "I want to write a book" was too vague. It wasn't until I changed my mindset and defined a concrete plan, "I will complete one chapter a month and finish my draft by November 15, 2025," that I finally gained momentum.

A goal without a plan is just a wish. Let's stop wishing and start building.

Define It So You Can Chase It

Saying "I want to be better" isn't a goal. It's a feeling. You've got to define what "better" looks like. Saving money? Name the amount and timeline. Rebuilding a relationship? Define the first step, maybe it's a phone call, not a miracle. Reclaiming your health? Identify what wellness looks like for *you*.

Vague goals blur movement. Clear goals give direction. And direction fuels action.

Set S.M.A.R.T. Goals

I remember sitting in a classroom years ago when an instructor introduced the concept of **S.M.A.R.T**. goals. That single framework stuck with me and has shaped every goal I've set since.

Here's what it stands for:

- **S**pecific – Name the exact outcome you're after.
- **M**easurable – Track your progress so you can celebrate it.
- **A**chievable – Stretch yourself, but stay grounded.
- **R**elevant – Make sure it aligns with what truly matters to you.
- **T**ime-bound – Put a clock on it. Deadlines drive discipline.

I still remember sitting in that classroom when I first heard about S.M.A.R.T. goals. That framework became a compass guiding every goal I've set since.

Example: Vague goal: "I want to go back to school."

S.M.A.R.T. goal: "I will enroll at the University of Alabama, take two online evening classes by August, and complete my associate degree in business administration within two years."

The first goal sounds good, but it doesn't tell you what success looks like or how you'll get there. The second one? That's real. It's got a plan, a timeline, and steps you can actually take. That's the difference between talking about it and being about it.

That's not a dream. That's a mission.

Attach It to Something That Matters

Want your goal to survive the hard days? Then you've got to give it a heartbeat.

As a Drill Sergeant, I would provide each new group of Soldiers with a 3×5 card and instruct them:

"Write down three reasons why you chose to attend Basic Training. There will be challenging days when it may feel easier to quit. This card is intended to serve as your anchor. If the reasons you have listed do not provide sufficient motivation to persevere, then you may need to reconsider your answers. Reflect deeply and write something that will sustain you during difficult times."

The same rule applies to your personal goals.

If your *why* doesn't light a fire in you, it won't carry you when the storms come.

I didn't start this book just because it sounded good. I started it because someone out there needs a nudge. A truth. A brotherhood of words.

Purpose gives your goal legs to stand on, even when your energy is low.

Map the Mission with Milestones

Big goals can feel intimidating. That's why we break them down.

My grandfather had a saying: "It's hard by the yard, but a cinch by the inch."

What he meant was simple: big goals can feel overwhelming when you look at the whole picture, but when you break it down and handle it one step at a time, it becomes manageable. Whether you're building a business, rewriting your mindset, or pushing through Basic Training, progress happens in inches. The key is consistency, not intensity.

He was right. When I committed to writing this book, I didn't sit down and knock it all out in one weekend. I started with one question: *What do I want this book to be about?*

Then came the outline. Then, I blocked Sunday mornings for writing my quiet window before the house wakes up.

Each step is stacked. Each moment mattered. And those wins? I celebrated them. Small victories spark momentum.

Stop waiting for the finish line to cheer; celebrate each mile marker as if it were a victory. Every step forward means you didn't quit, and that grind deserves respect. Don't just honor the end goal; honor the journey that's pushing you there.

Closing Thoughts

If your vision is still a blur, don't worry. Clarity comes with movement.

By now, you've faced your comfort zone. You've named your fears. And you've started reshaping your mindset. Now it's time to get precise.

- Write the goal.
- Define the mission.
- Attach it to something that fuels you.

The compass is set. The direction is clear. What's left is movement.

This next step? It won't be perfect. But it will be yours.

Because forward doesn't wait for flawless. It waits for *real*.

Let's drop the need for perfect plans and embrace *imperfect progress*. The kind that feels messy but moves mountains.

Ready or not, lace up and let's **Be about it.**

Reflection & Action

Target Locked: Before you move on, sharpen the aim. A strong goal creates strong movement.

1. What's one specific goal you want to accomplish in the next 3–6 months?

_____

_____

_____

_____

2. Why does this goal matter to you? What purpose does it serve?

_____

_____

_____

_____

Break your goal into three small, actionable steps, and you can start this week.

_____

_____

_____

_____

How will you celebrate progress along the way? Big or small, what will your reward look like?

_____

_____

_____

_____

CHAPTER FIVE

PROGRESS OVER PERFECTION: STRATEGIES FOR STARTING NOW, EVEN IF IT'S NOT PERFECT

"Start where you are. Use what you have. Do what you can." — **Arthur Ashe**

P erfection is a thief.

It talks a good game. It makes us wait. It whispers, "Not yet. You're not ready. Just one more tweak." But here's the truth: perfection doesn't build momentum. Progress does.

When I first thought about starting my business, *Don't Talk About It, Be About It Consulting, LLC,* I had no clue what I was doing. I had never owned a business. I didn't even know where to start. But once I stepped out on faith and began the process, things started to take shape. I made a lot of mistakes, but it was those mistakes that taught me the most valuable lessons.

A friend gave me the push I needed. He said, "Griff, stop waiting for the stars and moons to align. A 70 to 80 percent solution will get you a lot further than waiting for a perfect one."

And he was right. If I'd waited until everything was perfect, I'd still be standing still.

The Paralysis of Perfectionism

The desire to "get it right" can become the excuse to do nothing at all. And I hear it all the time.

I've watched smart, driven, purpose-filled people talk themselves out of greatness, not because they weren't capable, but because they didn't feel "ready." Waiting for the perfect time. The perfect setup. The perfect mood.

I've done it myself. And every time I gave in to that mindset, I stayed stuck.

You can research, plan, and prepare, but eventually, you have to press "go."

You can't build experience if you never begin.

Many people hesitate because they're afraid to fail. But failure isn't the enemy, it's the professor. I remember hearing Denzel Washington say, "If you're not failing, you're not even trying."

Somewhere along the way, we were taught that failure is shameful. But in truth, failure is a vital part of the process. Fail, and fail often. Just make sure every failure becomes a teaching moment, and you'll be just fine.

Progress isn't clean. It comes with trial, feedback, missteps, and lessons. But every step forward, even the wobbly ones, gets you closer to the person you're becoming.

"Done" Is a Muscle

Finishing things is discipline. It's a skill you build, and like any muscle, the more you use it, the stronger it gets.

Every time you complete a task, no matter how small, you remind yourself, *I can follow through. I can finish.*

Years ago, I developed a habit: if something took less than two minutes, I'd knock it out immediately. No delay. No circling back. That simple shift rewired my brain from "maybe later" to "handle it now."

Now, don't get me wrong, I've been a serial procrastinator at times. In fact, I used to thrive under pressure. But as I got older, I realized something: Finishing fresh reduces stress and compounds wins.

That's the mindset that helped me finish this book.

Start with small completions. Stack your momentum.

Celebrate Imperfect Progress

One of the biggest mistakes people make is saving the celebration for the finish line. That's a setup for burnout.

You have to celebrate the small wins along the way. They're the fuel that keeps your engine running.

I remember attending a four-month military course years ago. At the start, it felt like forever. But what made the difference were the weekly milestones. After each test, my classmates and I would celebrate. It wasn't just about the grade; it was about the progress.

Those celebrations built camaraderie. They built belief. And ultimately, they carried us through to graduation.

Progress deserves recognition.

Celebrate showing up. Celebrate being consistent. Celebrate learning something new, even if you're not where you want to be yet.

Course-Correct in Motion (The Pivot)

Ever try steering a parked car? Exactly. You can't.

You can't steer a parked vehicle, and you can't improve what isn't in motion.

The sooner you start moving, the sooner you can refine, adjust, and grow.

Some of the best decisions I've made didn't happen because I had all the answers. They happened because I trusted the next step. And with each move, the path got clearer.

When I first started writing this book, I had a completely different concept in mind.

But once I got in motion, I realized: *That's not the message I need to share right now.*

So, I pivoted.

And that's how *Don't Talk About It, Be About It* was born.

Now, if you're hoping I'll reveal that original concept, you'll have to wait for the next book. Come on now, I can't give away all the tools at once.

The point is this: you won't think your way into clarity; you've got to move your way into it.

Closing Thoughts

Perfection is the enemy of progress. You're done waiting for ideal conditions.

Forward motion is messy. It's real. It's powerful.

You don't need it all figured out. You just need to start.

Because when movement meets courage, momentum shows up. And once that momentum hits, it's hard to stop a mission that's already in motion.

You've kicked perfection to the curb and chosen progress. That's powerful.

But here's the next truth bomb: movement without structure leads to burnout. It's not just about getting things done; it's about getting the *right* things done.

That's where prioritization steps in. The next chapter gets tactical. It's about reclaiming your time, aligning your actions, and fueling your goals through rhythm and discipline. Because progress needs protection. And your purpose needs a plan.

Let's drop perfection.

Let's choose growth.

Let's *Be about it.*

Reflection & Action

Leaning Into Forward Motion: Take a breath. You've been waiting long enough. Let these questions shake loose the hesitation and awaken your next step. *

1. What's one thing you've delayed starting because it didn't feel "perfect" yet?

_____

_____

_____

_____

2. How has that delay affected your momentum or your mindset?

_____

_____

_____

_____

3. What small, imperfect action could you take in the next 24 hours to move forward?

_____

_____

_____

_____

4. How will you remind yourself that progress matters more than polish?

_____

_____

_____

_____

CHAPTER SIX

TIME MANAGEMENT AND PRIORITIZATION: TECHNIQUES FOR BALANCING COMPETING DEMANDS

"Don't tell me where your priorities are. Show me where you spend your time, and I'll tell you what they are." — James W. Frick

Time doesn't lie.

You can talk about what matters all day long, but your calendar will tell the truth. And for most people, that truth is hard to face.

We all get the same 24 hours. But not everyone uses them with purpose. Some waste them on distractions. Some give them away to everyone but themselves. And too many people think they're "too busy," when what they really are is unfocused.

Here's the reality: you don't find time. You make time.

When I was in the military, I learned fast that time is either your weapon or your weakness. As a Drill Sergeant, every second of the day was accounted for. If you missed your timeline, even by a minute, you might end up rucking fifteen miles instead of catching the bus to the range.

That taught me something: urgency doesn't equal readiness. You have to prepare before the clock starts ticking. I had to learn to command my time, not surrender it.

Let's dive in.

Audit Your Time Like You Audit Your Budget

Running a business taught me something I never truly learned in school: accountability lives in the details. Every dollar I spend, I track. Every expense is backed up. Why? Because if Uncle Sam comes knocking, I want my books clean.

Your time deserves that same respect.

When I tracked my time for the first time, I saw something ugly: I was giving away prime hours to things that drained me.

- Responding to every message
- Attending meetings with no purpose
- Binge-watching "just one more episode," then feeling wrecked the next morning.

The issue wasn't time; it was boundaries.

Your time tells a story. But you can't fix a story you won't read. So, take inventory:

- How much time do you lose to scrolling?
- How often do you pause your priorities to fix someone else's?
- When you say, "I'm busy," can you explain with what?

You'll be shocked by how much time leaks into what's loud but meaningless. Track it. Hour by hour. One week. No edits. No excuses. See it. Own it. Reclaim it.

Tools to Take Back Your Time

Sometimes, it's not that people lack drive. It's that they're spending their energy in the wrong direction. The truth is, if you don't know how to manage your time, your time will manage you.

Once you see where your time is going, it's time to reclaim those hours.

Here are two tools that helped me transition from confused motion to meaningful progress, without relying on complicated systems or expensive software.

The Eisenhower Matrix: The Mission Filter

In the Army, we analyzed every task. We knew what needed to happen now, what could wait, what belonged to someone else, and what didn't need to happen at all. The Eisenhower Matrix brings that same clarity to your everyday life:

- **Urgent & Important** → *Do it now* (This is non-negotiable. It must be done, and it must be done now. It's a thing that can't wait.)
- **Important but Not Urgent** → *Schedule it* (Your goals, going to the gym, your dreams; the quiet things that matter most.)
- **Urgent but Not Important** → *Delegate it* (That email notification. Someone asked for that favor at the last minute. It's loud, but not yours to carry.)

- **Not Urgent & Not Important** → *Eliminate it* (The scrolling on social media, the drama, and the distractions that don't serve your purpose.)

Eisenhower Matrix

	URGENT	NOT URGENT
URGANT	**IMPORTANT** DO IT NOW ↓	**IMPORTANT** SCHEDULE IT ↓
NOT IMPORTANT	**NOT IMPORTANT** DELEGATE IT ↓	**NOT IMPORTANT** ELIMINATE IT ↓

Every time I feel overwhelmed, I run my task list through this grid. It's like flipping on night vision goggles in the dark; suddenly, what matters most stands out with clarity.

Time Blocking: Assign Every Hour a Job

You can't steer a parked car. And you can't manage time you haven't given purpose to.

Time blocking means every hour has an assignment. Not rigid, but strategic.

Here's how mine looks:

- **Sunday Mornings** → Writing before the house wakes up.
- **Fridays at Noon** → Create reels for the organization.
- **Evenings** → Phone off. Family time. Recharge

When I block my time, I can actually be where my feet are. I'm not half-present, multitasking my way through mediocrity. I'm in it.

And when your goals live on your calendar, they stop being someday plans and start becoming everyday progress.

Protect What Matters Most

The final piece of time management isn't just about getting more done. It's about protecting the parts of your life that can't be outsourced. It's about setting boundaries and honoring them.

I used to say yes to everything: every meeting, every call, every opportunity. But over time, I realized I wasn't being generous. I was being drained. I was trading my peace for other people's priorities.

Here's what I've learned: your superpower is the word *"No."* Use it. Protect it. Respect it.

Because takers don't have limits. And if you keep saying yes, they will keep asking until there's nothing left. Now I ask better questions:

- Does this align with my values?
- Does this build or drain me?
- If I say yes to this… what am I silently saying no to?

Now, I schedule the things that recharge me before anything else:

- Morning devotions
- The gym
- Date night
- Quiet time
- Conversations that pour into me, not just pull from me.

People will test your boundaries, but no one else is responsible for protecting your peace. What matters to you will only survive if you protect it like the precious resource it is. Remember, self-love isn't selfish, it's necessary.

Time is the one currency you can never earn back; once it's spent, it's gone.

So, when you give your time, give it deliberately. Not everyone deserves a seat at your table, and not every invitation warrants a 'yes.' Boundaries aren't barriers — they're gates with a lock that only you control. Guard your time like your future depends on it…because it does.

Closing Thoughts

You've done the audit. You've learned the tools. You've named what matters. Now it's time to execute.

This isn't about grinding harder. It's about living in alignment with what matters.

It's about honoring your values with your calendar.

- Start today. Block one hour for you.
- Say no to what doesn't align.
- Build boundaries around what builds you up.

When you honor your schedule, you teach others to honor it too.

You've dialed in your schedule. You've prioritized your purpose. But here comes the next challenge: maintaining momentum when motivation fades.

Time management builds the frame. Accountability builds the walls.

Next up: how to surround yourself with truth-tellers, up-lifters, and mission-keepers who make sure you stay rooted, even when life shakes the ground.

And while you're at it... *Be about it.*

Reflection & Action

Schedule Your Strength: Time doesn't ask what matters to you. You have to tell it.

1. Where is your time going each day? List the biggest distractions.

_____

_____

_____

_____

2. What are 1–2 things that really matter to you, but keep getting crowded out?

_____

_____

_____

_____

3. Which task or habit belongs in each of these Eisenhower Matrix boxes?

Urgent & Important:

_____

_____

_____

_____

Important but Not Urgent:

_____

_____

_____

_____

Urgent but Not Important:

_____

_____

_____

_____

Not Urgent, Not Important:

_____

_____

_____

_____

_____

4. **Time Block**: What's one hour this week you can dedicate to your goal? What will you do with it?

_____

_____

_____

_____

CHAPTER SEVEN

BUILDING ACCOUNTABILITY AND SUPPORT: CREATING SYSTEMS THAT KEEP YOU ON MISSION

"Two are better than one… If either of them falls down, one can help the other up." — **Ecclesiastes 4:9–10 (NIV)**

Some journeys can't be taken solo.

You can build momentum. You can audit your time. You can block off goals on your calendar and be laser-focused. But eventually, life will test your grip. Distractions show up. Emotions get loud. Old habits start whispering, *"It's okay to pause."*

That's why discipline alone isn't enough.

You need people, the kind who don't just cheer when it's easy, but challenge you when it's not.

Accountability isn't a weakness; it's your armor.

It reminds you of your *why* when your feelings forget. It sharpens your edge when doubt shows up dull.

Let's talk about building the kind of community that keeps you on mission.

The Power of Being Seen

Sometimes all it takes is one person saying, "I see you trying, and I'm not going to let you quit."

Around Chapter 3 of this book, I hit a wall. I started second-guessing everything. Would my words even connect? Would anyone care? I was working in isolation, and when I stalled, there was no one to help me reset.

Then I made a decision: I shared my goal with people I trusted. And let me pause right here, because there's a difference between telling everyone and telling the right ones.

I've heard the phrase, "Keep your plans quiet until they're done." That's fine for some. But for me, I believe in being selective, not silent.

So, I brought my book journey to my Monday, Wednesday, and Friday morning motivation group. They didn't let me drift. They didn't just believe in the book; they believed in me. That accountability didn't just keep me moving, it kept me anchored.

Why? Because momentum responds to movement, and movement multiplies in a community.

The Right Circle Creates the Right Climate

Remember that "crab in a bucket" analogy from Chapter 1? One crab tries to rise, but the others pull it back. That wasn't just a metaphor about fear; it's a truth about environments.

Some circles will check your ego. But others? They'll contain your growth.

I remember going home on leave from the military. And each time, I felt less and less desire to do the things I used to do. What I realized was this: many of the people I'd grown up with were still in the same environment, same rhythms, same routines, and same mindset.

Me? I had changed. Not because I was better, but because I had been exposed to new things. The military expanded my view of life, discipline, and opportunity. It showed me there was more.

Exposure changes perspective. And once your lens shifts, your environment needs to follow.

If your circle rewards comfort but never challenges excuses... If your surroundings drain your discipline... It's time to upgrade your atmosphere.

Growth needs new soil. And your mission deserves a climate that cultivates it.

Types of Accountabilities That Work

Let's break this down. You don't need a boardroom of advisors. You need real people, clear roles, and intentional support.

As my grandfather used to say, "Closed mouths don't get fed." In other words, if you need backup, speak up.

Be honest. Be clear. Tell the people in your life exactly how they can support you, because no one can hold you accountable for something you never asked for.

During the COVID-19 pandemic, a few friends and I started a Facebook group that we called *The Council*. With everything shut down, that sense of connection and community had taken a hit. So, we made our own.

One video call turned into a tribe, comprising people from all over the world, from different walks of life, who brought ideas, accountability, and truth. There were no hidden agendas, and no one was trying to prove anything. Just a group of people ensuring we stayed good, grounded, and committed to what we had said we would do.

Five years later, *The Council* is still alive. Still just a phone call away. Still showing up.

Now hear me: I'm not telling you to go out and create your own group called *The Council,* but I am encouraging you to think about how you can build a support system that works for you.

Here are a few simple ways to get started:

Practical Accountability Strategies

- **The Weekly Check-in:** A quick 15-minute chat with a peer. One win. One challenge. One next step.
- **The Progress Thread:** A text group where you share small updates. Momentum loves company.
- **The Quiet Commitment:** Share your goal privately with someone who believes in you. Let them follow up in a week.

- **The Recap Ritual:** On Friday or Sunday, send a voice memo summarizing your week, including progress, reflection, and reset.

- **The "Push Me" Partner:** Find someone who's not impressed by comfort and will always ask, "What's next?" The goal isn't pressure; it's presence.

Someone who shows up for your progress, even when you want to pull back.

Build Your Board of Belief

In the military, I always knew who was on my left and right. We trained together. We hurt together. We won together. That same principle applies to your personal mission today.

You don't need a crowd. You need a crew.

That's why I encourage you to build what I call your *Board of Belief*, a small group of people who see you, sharpen you, and stay with you when the mission gets rough.

Your Board should include:

- **Truth-Teller:** For me, that was my mother. She never told me what I wanted to hear; she told me what I needed to hear to get back on track. Since her passing, that role has been filled by my wife and daughter. They don't hold back, and I'm grateful. As a former boss once said, "Feedback is a gift."

- **Vision-Voice:** The encourager who sees greatness in you, even when you can't.

- **Pathfinder:** A mentor, whether direct or distant, who has traveled the path and left footprints for you to follow. Learn from their wins, and just as importantly, from their wounds.

- **Steady Presence:** They might not talk much, but their actions say it all. This is your ride-or-die, the one who has stuck beside you through every season and still shows up when it counts.

You see, society wants you to believe you need a lot of followers, likes, and a platform. But the truth is, your mission doesn't need a fanbase. It needs a foundation.

It's not the number of people on your *Board of Belief* that counts. It's the quality that carries you forward.

Write down a few names. Reach out. Don't assume people know how to support you; invite them into the role.

Support Isn't Just for Struggle

Accountability isn't just about checking boxes; it's about celebrating the climb.

I've heard it said many times: "It's lonely at the top."

And I always respond: "Only if you don't bring someone with you."

Support isn't just for the struggle. It matters just as much in the win.

So let your people celebrate with you. When you finish a chapter, share it.

When you hit the gym five days in a row, say it out loud.

When you choose discipline over drama, toast it with a friend, with water, Gatorade, or your favorite drink. It doesn't matter.

What matters is this: you did it, and you brought someone with you to witness it.

Because what's the point of reaching a mountaintop if there's no one there to clap when you plant the flag?

Some folks will call it bragging. Let them. That's their business, not yours.

The right people? They'll celebrate with you and thank you for making them part of the moment.

The goal of support isn't just about accountability. It's about shared joy.

And momentum multiplies when others feel invested in your growth.

Closing Thoughts

Discipline gets you moving. But support? That's the anchor when your momentum starts to sway.

Don't just dream alone, build a crew that challenges, encourages, and stretches you. Don't grind in silence, share the progress, the setbacks, and the pivots. Show people what resilience really looks like. And when you climb out of the bucket, don't just get free, change the structure. Help someone else engineer their escape.

This isn't about applause or optics. You're crafting a life where accountability isn't optional; it's embedded. One that trades excuses for execution and comfort for clarity.

Because you don't just owe it to yourself to become, you owe it to the world to become visible.

So, while you're at it... be about it. Not for validation, because validation is for parked cars. But for transformation. And let your actions echo louder than any title ever could.

Reflection & Action

Call In the Right Voices: *"If you want to go fast, go alone. If you want to go far, go together."* — **African Proverb**

1. Who are the three people in your life who genuinely support your growth?

_____

_____

_____

_____

2. Who do you need to ask for honest feedback or accountability right now?

_____

_____

_____

_____

3. What's one area of your life or goal where you've been trying to go alone? Why?

_____

_____

_____

_____

4. When was the last time you invited someone to celebrate your progress with you? What would that look like this week?

_____

_____

_____

_____

FINAL THOUGHTS: BE ABOUT IT

You didn't just read a book. You walked through mindset shifts. You told the truth about your fear. You confronted your comfort zone. You dared to move without a perfect plan.

You audited your time, reclaimed your energy, and now you know who's walking with you.

Let me be clear: this was never about motivation. That fades. This was never about hype. That wears off. This was about waking something up inside of you that says:

I'm done watching from the sidelines.

I'm done blaming time, fear, or circumstances.

I'm done waiting for the right moment — because this moment is mine.

And now?

You don't need permission.

You don't need one more plan.

You just need to remember who you are. You are action.

You are disciplined.

You are a legacy in motion.

So, whatever's next, launch the vision, finish the goal, take the step…

And always remember, *Don't Talk about It, Be About It.*

Final Reflection & Commitment

Be About It. Starting Now: *Reading inspires. Action transforms.*

1. What was your biggest truth revealed in these pages?

_____

_____

_____

_____

2. What will you stop doing today that's held you back?

_____

_____

_____

_____

3. What will you start doing to show up as the best version of you?

_____

_____

_____

_____

_____

4. What's one bold action you commit to within the next 7 days?

_____

_____

_____

_____

Write it down. Sign it. Be about it.

✎ Signature: _____

🖊 Date: _____

This isn't the end. It's ignition. You've read it. You've reflected on it. Now go and act.

The End

Notes

_____

_____

_____

_____

_____

_____

_____

_____

_____

_____

_____

_____

_____

_____

_____

_____

_____

_____

_____

_____

_____

_____

_____

_____

_____

_____

_____

_____

_____

_____

_____

_____

_____

_____

_____

_____

_____

_____

_____

_____

_____

_____

_____

_____

_____

_____

_____

ABOUT THE AUTHOR

Garrick Griffin is a proud native of Birmingham, Alabama. Raised in a single-parent household alongside his brother in a low-income housing community, he was surrounded by something far greater than wealth, unshakable love, and support.

He joined the United States Army in 1990 and served with distinction for over 30 years, culminating his career as the Command Sergeant Major of Fort Knox Garrison. Garrick holds a Master of Science in Management from Excelsior College and a Bachelor of General Studies from Columbia College. He is also a member of the Maxwell Leadership Certified Team, equipping leaders across the world with tools to influence and inspire.

After retirement, Garrick founded *Don't Talk About It, Be About It Consulting, LLC,* a coaching and leadership development firm committed to helping individuals and teams lead with action, authenticity, and accountability.

He believes that leadership is not about titles, it's about

action. His mission is simple: help others lead themselves first, then lead with impact.

Known for his commanding presence, authentic storytelling, and hard-earned wisdom, Garrick speaks to audiences ranging from corporate teams to military units, inspiring them to trade excuses for execution.

Whether coaching, speaking, or serving behind the scenes, Garrick continues to live out his message every day: *Don't talk about it, Be About It.*

He is married to his lifelong partner, Mrs. Earline Griffin, and together they are the proud parents of three sons, Darius, Garrick II, and the late Daquan, and one daughter, Myka Rai-Lynn. His family remains his greatest joy, his deepest motivation, and his daily reminder of what legacy truly means.

Connect with the Author

Thank you for walking with me through *Don't Talk About It, Be About It.*

This book was written to spark action, honor legacy, and remind us that leadership begins with accountability.

If something in these pages moved you, challenged you, or aligned with your mission, let's keep the conversation going.

✉ **Email:** garrick.griffin43@gmail.com

📞 **Phone:** 346-827-5212

🌐 **Website:** www.donttalkaboutit.net

▨ **Facebook:** Don't Talk About It, Be About It Consulting

www.ingramcontent.com/pod-product-compliance
Lightning Source LLC
Chambersburg PA
CBHW051642120626
46551CB00014B/2178